A GUIDE TO
COMPANION
PLANTING

Michael Littlewood

Published by
Michael Littlewood
PO Box 25
South Petherton
Somerset TA13 5WZ

ISBN: 978-0-9563628-0-3

Edited by Gaby Bartai

Designed by Andrew Crane

*Right: Calendula (pot marigold) makes one of the best
all-round companions. Picture: Dave Bevan*

Contents

Companion planting benefits

- *Attracts beneficial insects to the garden*

- *Supports stronger, healthier plant growth*

- *Increases crop yields*

- *Discourages pests*

- *Reduces plant diseases*

- *Discourages weeds*

- *Replaces the use of garden chemicals*

- *Creates a valuable habitat for wildlife*

- *Benefits the wider environment*

- *Saves the gardener time and money*

- *Makes the garden more attractive, interesting and rewarding*

1 | INTRODUCTION

A conventional approach thinks of the garden as a series of separate compartments. Vegetables are grown in one distinct area, and flowers in another – often separated by the house into 'back' and 'front' gardens. The herb garden may be in a special plot of its own, and fruit trees and soft fruit often have their own distinct areas. In the vegetable plot, crops are separated into long rows or large blocks, each of a single species.

Companion planting overturns this mindset. It is part of a holistic approach to gardening which recognises that everything is interconnected, and which asks us to see the garden – and the environment beyond it – as a whole. It invites us to grow herbs and flowers amongst our vegetables and fruit, and to abandon large blocks or long rows of individual crops in favour of mixed planting.

In this plot, companion flowers and flowering herbs are grown amongst the vegetables, and insect-attracting weeds have been allowed to flourish at the edges of the bed. Picture: Michael Littlewood

Here, the vegetables are grown in traditionally sterile rows, and flowers are relegated to a separate area.
Picture: Michael Littlewood

The result will be a healthier, more productive garden, which thrives because it is working in harmony with nature.

Companion planting can improve plant health, increase crop yields, deter pests, discourage weeds, reduce the incidence of diseases, and attract beneficial insects. The garden will become a valuable wildlife habitat, which is of benefit to the gardener as well as to wildlife, because pest species will largely be controlled by natural predators. This means that the use of pesticides can be abandoned, which will save you money, reduce your workload, and further benefit the environment. Companion planting is part of the organic approach to gardening, and will only produce good results within an organic system. Working with nature is incompatible with the use of garden chemicals, which work against it.

The term 'companion planting' describes the planting together of two or more species for the benefit of one, both or all of them. In its broader sense, it describes the grouping together of plants that make good neighbours. In its widest sense, it describes any interaction between plants where one can be said to be having an effect on another.

It can refer to the pairing up of two specific plants for a specific purpose – discouraging a particular pest, for example. It also encompasses intercropping, where two crops are grown together with more general benefits in mind, and mixed planting, where a range of crops and companion plants are grown as a community. Companion planting generally involves growing flowers and herbs with vegetables or fruit, but there are also some specific associations between pairs of vegetables.

Companion planting can be incorporated into any size or style of garden, and although it is now the subject of serious scientific research, its basic principles and applications are not arcane or complicated. Many companion planting techniques are straightforward and easy to put into practice, even for new gardeners. The addition of flowers and herbs to a vegetable plot or orchard will make it a more beautiful, fulfilling and therapeutic place to work, and whatever your level of skill and experience, it will make growing edible crops even more interesting and rewarding.

Flowers with a simple, open structure, like these annual chrysanthemums, will attract beneficial insects.
Picture: Michael Littlewood

2 | THE HISTORY OF COMPANION PLANTING

Observations of companion planting effects go back to classical times. Although the use of some horticultural chemicals goes back just as far, for the most part our ancestors relied on planting techniques to give them good results – and success was vital, since crop failure could mean famine. They learnt through careful observation, and their accumulated knowledge was passed down from generation to generation.

Varro, who lived in the third century BC, noted that walnut trees made the surrounding ground sterile, and that vines did not do well near cabbages. Two hundred years later, Columella recommended interplanting cabbages, globe artichokes, lettuces and radishes with vetches, onions and wormwood, observing that the crops would then not be troubled by pests, especially caterpillars. In the first century AD, Pliny wrote of plants exuding scents or juices that harmed competing plants. All of these are sound observations which are incorporated into modern companion planting practice.

Monastic gardens preserved classical gardening traditions through the Dark and Middle Ages, and companion planting resurfaces in the Elizabethan idea of 'barrier planting', in which rows of

Left: Leave surplus vegetables like these onions and parsnips to flower – they make excellent insect-attractants. Picture: Michael Littlewood

vegetables were separated by strips of appropriate companion herbs. For instance, rows of lettuces and peas were separated by strips of garlic or chives to prevent insect attack, and nasturtiums were planted between rows of broccoli. Herbs including hyssop, rosemary, sage and thyme were used to deter aphids and cabbage white butterflies, and these were traditionally planted between rows of cabbages.

Lettuce rows alternated with chives and poached egg plants – an example of 'barrier planting'. Picture: Dave Bevan

By the 18th century, French market gardeners had developed methods of interplanting a number of different crops in order to maximise the yield from their ground. They are recorded as having grown cabbages, cauliflower, celery and lettuces together; another companion group was endives, onions, spinach, strawberries and turnips. Meanwhile, the typical private 'cottage garden' was a riotous mix of flowers, medicinal herbs and fruit.

The science of companion planting began to emerge in 1924, when Rudolf Steiner laid the foundations for the biodynamic method of

Rudolf Steiner

agriculture, and much of the subsequent research into the subject has been the work of biodynamic growers. Today, some mainstream scientific establishments are beginning to research companion planting, but their investigations tend to be limited to crops and partnerships that have possible commercial applications.

This means that much of what we know about companion planting is the result of experimentation by individuals working in their private gardens. It is a huge and fascinating subject, and what we know so far is only the tip of the iceberg. Companion planting is an evolving science, and much of it will continue to be developed on the ground by ordinary gardeners. Enthusiasts can become part of a unique, ongoing experiment that makes growing edible crops even more interesting and rewarding.

Right: Ornamental mixed planting at Cockington Court in Devon. Picture: Cockington Court

3 | GARDENING WITH NATURE
The benefits of mixed cropping

In natural conditions, plants grow in close communities with a number of different species existing side by side. Plants thrive when huddled together, protecting one another from the stresses of weather and climate. The antithesis of this natural way of growing is monoculture, where plants are grown in large blocks of single species – as practised on most farms, in intensive commercial gardens, and in many conventional private gardens. This is the least healthy system of cultivation, because it makes life very easy for species-specific pests and diseases. In the absence of any natural predators – because there are no companion plants to attract and support them – growers reach for the spray gun.

Mixed planting, mimicking natural growing systems, creates greater biodiversity, which in turn creates much more stability and resilience in the face of changing conditions. Instead of the endless feast provided by a conventional planting scheme, mixed planting forces pests to hunt for their next meal, which is probably some distance away – and locating it is made more difficult by the confusing scents of the many different plants *en route*. This technique is very effective in minimising insect damage to your crops.

Left: Here, the crops are grown in traditional rows, but the planting is dense and mixed.
Picture: Michael Littlewood

The more mixed the planting, the better – but truly mixed cropping can be difficult to manage. Interplanting two or three different crops in each area of your plot may be an easier way forward. If you are growing a large amount of one crop, it is better to plant several small areas in different parts of your garden than to plant a single large block.

Interplanting: leeks and strawberries, with a seedling green manure crop alongside them. Picture: Michael Littlewood

Plant families

Garden vegetables belong to a number of different plant families, and these families are, in general, natural companions, appreciating the same growing conditions and growing well together. Peppers and aubergines, for instance, are 'good companions' because they both like warm, moist conditions. It is often – although not always – the case that vegetables from different families are 'bad companions' because they need different conditions, or because one would create growing conditions detrimental to the other.

The grouping of vegetables into plant families extends into the important principle of crop rotation, whereby each family is grown together, and the families are moved around the garden each year. By dividing your vegetable garden into several sections of the same size, you can move the families around the plot in a cyclical pattern, so that each only returns to its original plot after a gap of several years. This means that pests and diseases specific to particular families do not get a chance to build up in the soil. It also makes effective use of soil nutrients, because the different crop families make different demands on the soil.

Crop rotation can be regarded as 'companion planting over time', because a rotation sequence is worked out so that each crop benefits from the conditions left by the previous occupants of that plot, and leaves conditions beneficial to the next. For instance, it works well to grow brassicas (the cabbage family) in a plot where legumes (peas and beans) grew the previous year, because legumes have the ability to 'fix' nitrogen from the atmosphere, leaving the surplus in the soil, and brassicas have a high nitrogen requirement.

Most organic authorities agree that it is important to follow a crop rotation, and to avoid growing vegetables from the different plant families together. This can sometimes conflict with

It is best to keep the different crop families separate; here, the cabbage family is being grown together, with the potatoes in a separate area behind them.
Picture: Dave Bevan

companion planting advice – for instance, it is sometimes suggested that you interplant brassicas with French or broad beans. It may be better to stick to companion planting with herbs and flowers, and avoid interplanting vegetables from the different families. However, some vegetables, notably most salad crops, do not belong to any of the major plant families, and these can safely be grown alongside vegetables from any of the main families.

The key exception to the rule about growing crop families together concerns potatoes and tomatoes. These are susceptible to the same diseases and can cross-infect one another, so should be kept apart.

The principle of growing naturally companionable plants together can be put into practice in other ways. Some suggested companion pairings are based on the fact that the two crops have complementary nutrient needs, enabling them to grow together without competing. A pairing may, for instance, suggest putting a deep-rooting plant alongside a shallow-rooting one, so that they take nutrients from different depths. Or it may suggest interplanting two crops – lettuces and cabbages, for instance – on the grounds that one will be harvested ahead of the other. This makes efficient use of space in the short term, and by the time the longer-term crop needs the extra growing space, the other crop will have been harvested.

Crop plant families

Apiaceae	• carrot, celeriac, celery, fennel, lovage, parsley, parsnip
Brassicaceae ('brassicas')	• broccoli, Brussels sprout, cabbage, calabrese, cauliflower, kale, kohlrabi, mustard, radish, rocket, swede, turnip
Chenopodiaceae	• beetroot, spinach, Swiss chard
Cucurbitaceae ('cucurbits')	• courgette, cucumber, marrow, melon, pumpkin, squash
Liliaceae ('alliums')	• asparagus, chives, garlic, leek, onion, shallot
Papilionaceae ('legumes')	• broad bean, French bean, pea, runner bean
Solanaceae	• aubergine, chilli, pepper, potato, tomato

Common vegetables and salads not listed here belong to other families and can be grouped with vegetables from any of the plant families above.

4 | SPECIFIC COMPANION BENEFITS

If you are new to companion planting, intercropping and mixed planting provide an easy way in. They offer many of its general benefits without any of the planning that is involved in researching and implementing specific companion plant pairings. Once you are familiar with the basic principles, however, it is time to investigate the further benefits that are offered by specific planting associations.

Companion effects

- *Plants can attract beneficial insects*
- *Plants can confuse or repel pests*
- *Plants can distract pests from other plants*
- *Plants can reduce the incidence of diseases in other plants*
- *Plants can improve soil fertility*
- *Plants can help to feed other plants*
- *Plants can cater to the physical needs of other plants*
- *Plants can compete with one another*
- *Plants can inhibit the growth of other plants*

Left: Nasturtiums provide a companion border for
this salad bed. Picture: Michael Littlewood

Plants that attract pollinators and predators

If you attract pollinating insects to your garden, they are likely to stay and pollinate vegetable crops like runner beans. Picture: Dave Bevan

Any plant that attracts beneficial insects to the garden can be regarded as a general-purpose 'good companion'. Our gardens are valuable, and increasingly vital, resources for wildlife, and growing a range of companion plants which are attractive to insects will ensure that they become biodiverse, thriving wildlife habitats. This is also of enormous benefit to the gardener.

Many of our crops, including almost all fruits, berries and nuts, and many vegetables, rely on insect pollination to produce a crop. It is therefore vital that sufficient pollinating insects are present in our gardens at the right time. Planting suitable flowers and herbs amongst or alongside these crops will attract any pollinating insects in the vicinity,

and once in your garden they are likely to spot and pollinate your crops. This is especially important at the beginning and end of the season, when natural food sources for insects can be scarce, and it is of course essential to match the flowering time of the companion plants to the flowering time of your crops.

Good choices are poached egg plant, phacelia, calendula (pot marigold), alpine strawberries, buckwheat and flowering herbs, but there are endless possibilities. The important thing is that the flowers have a simple, open structure, making the nectar and pollen easily accessible. Avoid highly bred, double or multi-petalled cultivars and hybrids, which often have inaccessible nectar and pollen – or none at all.

These companion plants will also attract predatory and parasitic insects, such as hoverflies, lacewings and parasitic wasps. Once in the garden, they and their larvae will prey on pest populations, reducing crop damage. Flowering herbs, especially the umbelliferous herbs, which include coriander, dill, fennel and parsley, are particularly good choices here, as are members of the daisy family such as feverfew and yarrow.

Remember that birds are also important natural pest controllers; growing a range of seed- and berry-bearing plants will entice more of them to your garden, so this too can be regarded as a form of companion planting.

Plants that help with pest control

Many insect pests locate their target plants by scent, and growing other, stronger-scented plants nearby can be an effective method of protecting vulnerable crops. This sometimes works by masking the scent of the crop plant, and sometimes by repelling the insects; these effects overlap, and it is not always clear which is in play.

Aromatic herbs with a high volatile oil content, like mint, lavender and rosemary, seem to work by

Onions are a traditional companion for carrots, deterring carrot root fly. Picture: Dave Bevan

confusing insect pests or disguising the scent of the target plants. Others, like the alliums (the onion family) and very pungent herbs like wormwood, seem to exude substances that are distasteful to pests. These exudations permeate the surrounding area, so that nearby plants are not touched by pests, or may even be absorbed into the tissues of nearby plants, so that they themselves become distasteful. Other natural insect repellents include asters, autumn chrysanthemums, cosmos, coreopsis and the *Tanacetum* genus, which includes pyrethrum, tansy and feverfew.

The most famous example of scent confusion is the use of onions to hide the scent of carrots from carrot fly. Trials by Garden Organic and the University of Cambridge have established that this works – though with provisos. The onions have to be in active growth – it no longer works once they start to form bulbs – and there need to be four times as many onions as carrots. Chives and chervil are also said to disguise the scent of carrots, and the organic gardening authority Joy Larkcom suggests mixing your carrot seed with the seed of strongly-scented annual flowers.

Another well-researched pairing is French marigolds (*Tagetes*) alongside tomatoes, particularly in the greenhouse, to discourage whitefly. It is important to realise that these effects can be very specific; marigolds, for instance, have no effect against carrot fly. Other well-known examples include nasturtiums, which can be grown up and over apple trees to drive away woolly aphids, and the use of alliums, especially garlic, to deter aphids. Flea beetles are said to be discouraged from infesting brassicas if tomatoes are grown alongside them, and lavender, rosemary and tansy are said to deter cabbage white butterflies.

If the idea of planting specific companions alongside specific crops seems too daunting, companion planting for pest control can be introduced in a more general way. Planting a range of 'deterrent' companion plants amongst or alongside your vegetables will go a long way towards reducing pest damage. The more 'repellent' plants there are in your garden, the less insects will feel that it is the ideal place to live and breed.

Visual confusion

Companion planting can also be used to confuse pests which detect their host plant by sight. The most extensively researched example of this is brassicas, interplanted with French or broad beans or underplanted with clover. This has been shown to reduce cabbage white butterfly caterpillars by a third. The reason this works is that the butterflies locate brassicas by searching for the outline of the foliage against the ground. By removing the contrast between brassicas and soil, you can camouflage your crop.

Nasturtiums, grown up and around apple trees, will help to deter woolly aphids. Picture: Michael Littlewood

Sacrificial plants

Some companion plants can be grown as 'sacrificial' or 'trap' plants, the idea being that they are more attractive to particular pests than the plants you want to protect. For instance, you can grow nasturtiums or hyssop to entice cabbage white butterflies away from brassicas. Basil will draw aphids away from neighbouring crops, so is traditionally grown alongside greenhouse crops like tomatoes and aubergines. Lettuce, spinach and other soft seedlings can be sown to distract slugs from other, tougher plants. Red spider mites prefer broad beans to any other crop, so beans can be planted beneath vulnerable, high-value crops like peaches. Flowers like *Nicotiana* (tobacco plant) or calendula can be grown in pots in the greenhouse to lure aphids; the trap plants can then be periodically dispatched to the compost heap and replaced, leaving your crops aphid-free.

However, this strategy is not without its risks. Insect populations tend to rise in response to the available food supply, and once their favourite plants are exhausted, they will move on to any other suitable plants nearby, including your crops. It is therefore vital that you ensure a continuous supply of the sacrificial plants.

Nasturtiums will distract cabbage white butterflies from brassicas, so your cabbages stay caterpillar-free. Picture: Sally Cunningham

Plants that prevent disease

Some plants have been found to be effective against fungal diseases. The best-known of these is garlic; a spray made from garlic is a known fungicide, and the growing plant also has a protective effect. Garlic is traditionally grown beneath fruit trees to prevent fungal diseases (and beneath roses to prevent blackspot), and chives are said to deter scab on apple trees. Strawberries are said to be less susceptible to fungal diseases – and to fruit and taste better into the bargain – if borage is grown nearby. Other plants with known anti-fungal properties include stinging nettles and horsetail (*Equisetum*).

Equisetum is a pernicious weed – but it does have companion benefits.

Current research is also finding that disease-susceptible vegetable varieties can be protected by interplanting them with disease-resistant varieties of the same species. Trials have shown, for instance, that lettuce susceptible to powdery mildew can be protected from attack if the plants are alternated with lettuces of a variety resistant to the disease. This technique might offer us a way of growing disease-susceptible heritage cultivars successfully.

Chives protect nearby plants from fungal diseases. Picture: Dave Bevan

Plants that improve the soil

Many plants in the legume family, such as peas, beans and clovers, have the ability to 'fix' nitrogen from the atmosphere. This is stored in nodules on their roots, and when they die, the surplus is left in the soil and benefits subsequent crops. Adding clover to a lawn-seed mixture, for instance, will improve the health of the grass. Clover can also be underplanted beneath tall crops like sweet corn or brassicas to keep the ground cool, moist and weed-free. After the crop has been harvested, the clover can be left to protect the soil during the winter, and in the spring it can be dug into the ground, where its nutrients will be released to feed other plants.

Other plants can be used to improve soil texture and structure for the benefit of subsequent crops. A number of green manures – plants which are grown specifically to improve the soil – fall into this category. Varieties with extensive, penetrating root systems, like alfalfa (also known as lucerne), buckwheat, grazing rye and lupins, can be used to break up a heavy soil. Mustard exudes alkaline secretions from its roots and can be used to prepare an acidic soil for a crop which prefers more alkaline conditions.

Plants from the legume family, like fenugreek (on the left), are valuable companions because they 'fix' nitrogen from the atmosphere. Picture: Sally Cunningham

Plants that help to feed others

Deep-rooting plants, including comfrey, green manures like alfalfa, and weeds like docks, dredge up nutrients from the subsoil which are beyond the reach of virtually all crop plants, and some plants take up specific minerals from the soil in greater than normal quantities. If these 'accumulator' plants are then composted, dug back into the soil, used as a mulch or made into a liquid feed, the nutrients can be passed on to our crops. This can also be regarded as a 'companion' effect.

Nurse crops

Some companion effects are straightforwardly physical. Many plants require shelter from wind, shade from excessive sunshine, or support to grow up, and these needs can sometimes be met by other plants. By this definition, a hedge can be regarded as companion planting, providing a windbreak to shelter the plants within a garden. On a smaller scale, tender crops like courgettes and pumpkins can be planted in the lee of robust, hardier plants, like Jerusalem artichokes or runner beans. On a smaller scale still, you can sow seeds, or transplant seedlings, in the lee of established plants.

The shade cast by tall crops is often a negative companion effect, but it can be turned to your advantage if you plant crops like lettuce and spinach, which will quickly run to seed in full summer sun, on the north side of them. Tall sturdy plants like sunflowers or sweet corn can act as living plant supports for twining crops like climbing French beans, and shrubby plants can also be used to support climbers.

Sow seeds between established crops for a 'nurse' companion effect. Picture: Michael Littlewood

The 'three sisters': squash, sweet corn and beans. Picture: Dave Bevan

Some plants can provide one another with mutually beneficial physical conditions. A good example of this is the 'three sisters' – squash, sweet corn and climbing beans, a trio of companion plants traditionally grown together by Native American gardeners. The dense growth of the squash plants keeps the ground moist and shaded, which suits the corn and the beans; the corn and beans act as windbreaks for the squash; the corn provides support for the beans; and the beans 'fix' nitrogen, which feeds all three plants.

5 | NEGATIVE COMPANION EFFECTS

Competition

Although plants naturally grow closely together, they are also in competition with one another for light, water, nutrients and space. In natural conditions, this will result in some plants becoming dominant and others being edged out, as the stronger species outgrow and outshade their competitors. In a garden, we need to ensure that all our plants are given sufficient space so that competition for resources does not become an issue between them.

We also need to implement effective measures of weed control so that native plants do not outcompete the ones we are trying to grow. One strategy is to turn competition between plants to your advantage. By sowing a low-growing green manure like clover beneath a crop, or interplanting two vegetables at close spacing, you can use companion planting to crowd out weeds.

Growth inhibitors

Some plants have developed an additional strategy to use against their competitors: they give off chemicals which inhibit the growth of other plants. These 'exudates', secreted by the leaves and/or roots of the plant, are known as 'allelopathic'.

Some plants release chemicals which prevent their own seedlings germinating beneath them, so the parent plant is not threatened by competition

Left: Companion planting in the Biodynamic Garden at Garden Organic Ryton in Warwickshire. Picture: Michael Littlewood

during its lifetime. With some species the effect persists after the parent plant dies or is removed. This is encountered in the garden as 'replant disease', notably in apples and roses, which leave chemicals in the soil which poison other plants of the same species. If you remove an apple or a rose, you should not plant another on the same site.

Other plants release chemicals which inhibit the growth of other species. The walnut, for instance, produces the poisonous chemical juglone, which inhibits most competing vegetation. Some herbs, including wormwood, fennel, rue, sage, rosemary and lavender, appear to inhibit seed germination, probably through exudates from fallen leaves. These herbs are therefore best kept away from areas of your garden where you are planning to grow crops from seed. If you want to grow them nearby for their other benefits, confine them to the edges of your plot.

There are also some known negative effects between specific pairs of vegetables. Broad beans and peas are inhibited by members of the onion family. Tomato root exudates have been shown to inhibit cucumber plants, and broccoli inhibits the growth of a subsequent cauliflower crop. This is a relatively new area of research, and there are doubtless many more examples yet to be discovered. Where a plant appears to be having an effect on another that cannot be explained otherwise, leaf or root exudations are a likely reason.

Some green manure crops, notably buckwheat, tares and grazing rye, inhibit seed germination as they decompose. This is a negative companion effect if you attempt to follow them with a crop from seed – but you can turn it to your advantage, because they also suppress weed growth. If you instead plant potato tubers, onion sets or pot-raised seedlings there, your crop will be able to establish itself without significant competition from weeds.

Another positive application of allelopathy involves the use of Mexican marigold *Tagetes minuta* to help clear ground infested with pernicious weeds. Its root secretions can assist in killing a range of weeds including ground elder, horsetail and bindweed, and it is also effective in controlling harmful nematodes.

Rue inhibits the germination of nearby seeds – so it is best kept away from potential seed-beds. Picture: Dave Bevan

Specific plant associations

Companion Planting Chart by Michael Littlewood available from www.ecodesignscape.co.uk

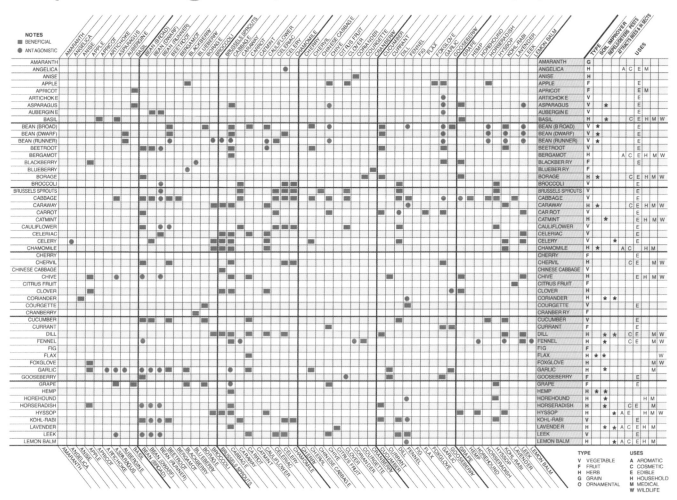

NOTES
■ BENEFICIAL
● ANTAGONISTIC

Plant	TYPE	SOIL IMPROVER	REPELS SYSTEM. PESTS	ATTRACTS BEES & INSECTS	USES
AMARANTH	G				
ANGELICA	H				A C E M
ANISE	H				
APPLE	F				E
APRICOT	F				E M
ARTICHOKE	V				E
ASPARAGUS	V	★			E
AUBERGINE	V				E
BASIL	H	★			C E H M W
BEAN (BROAD)	V	★			E
BEAN (DWARF)	V	★			E
BEAN (RUNNER)	V	★			E
BEETROOT	V				E
BERGAMOT	H				A C E H M W
BLACKBERRY	F				E
BLUEBERRY	F				
BORAGE	H	★			C E H M W
BROCCOLI	V				E
BRUSSELS SPROUTS	V				E
CABBAGE	V				E
CARAWAY	H	★			C E H M W
CARROT	V				E
CATMINT	H	★			C E H M W
CAULIFLOWER	V				E
CELERIAC	V				E
CELERY	V	★			E
CHAMOMILE	H	★			A C H M
CHERRY	F				E
CHERVIL	H				C E M W
CHINESE CABBAGE	V				
CHIVE	H				E H M W
CITRUS FRUIT	F				
CLOVER	H				
CORIANDER	H	★ ★			
COURGETTE	V				E
CRANBERRY	F				
CUCUMBER	V				E
CURRANT	F				E
DILL	H	★ ★			C E M W
FENNEL	H	★			C E M W
FIG	F				
FLAX	H	★ ★			W
FOXGLOVE	H				M W
GARLIC	H	★			M
GOOSEBERRY	F				E
GRAPE	F	★			E
HEMP	H	★ ★			
HOREHOUND	H				H M
HORSERADISH	H	★			C E M
HYSSOP	H	★	A E		H M W
KOHL-RABI	V				E
LAVENDER	H	★ ★	A		C E H
LEEK	V				C E H M
LEMON BALM	H		A	C E H M	

Column headers (top, diagonal): AMARANTH, ANGELICA, ANISE, APPLE, APRICOT, ARTICHOKE, ASPARAGUS, AUBERGINE, BASIL, BEAN (BROAD), BEAN (DWARF), BEAN (RUNNER), BEETROOT, BERGAMOT, BLACKBERRY, BLUEBERRY, BORAGE, BROCCOLI, BRUSSELS SPROUTS, CABBAGE, CARAWAY, CARROT, CATMINT, CAULIFLOWER, CELERIAC, CELERY, CHAMOMILE, CHERRY, CHERVIL, CHINESE CABBAGE, CHIVE, CITRUS FRUIT, CLOVER, CORIANDER, COURGETTE, CRANBERRY, CUCUMBER, CURRANT, DILL, FENNEL, FIG, FLAX, FOXGLOVE, GARLIC, GOOSEBERRY, GRAPE, HEMP, HOREHOUND, HORSERADISH, HYSSOP, KOHL-RABI, LAVENDER, LEEK, LEMON BALM

TYPE		USES	
V	VEGETABLE	A	AROMATIC
F	FRUIT	C	COSMETIC
H	HERB	E	EDIBLE
G	GRAIN	H	HOUSEHOLD
O	ORNAMENTAL	M	MEDICAL
		W	WILDLIFE

Companion Planting Chart © Michael Littlewood

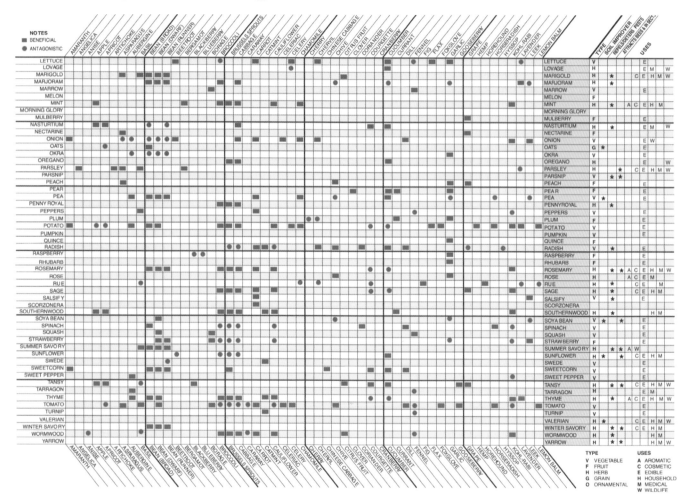

NOTES
- ■ BENEFICIAL
- ● ANTAGONISTIC

TYPE
- V VEGETABLE
- F FRUIT
- H HERB
- G GRAIN
- O ORNAMENTAL

USES
- A AROMATIC
- C COSMETIC
- E EDIBLE
- H HOUSEHOLD
- M MEDICAL
- W WILDLIFE

Companion Planting Chart © Michael Littlewood

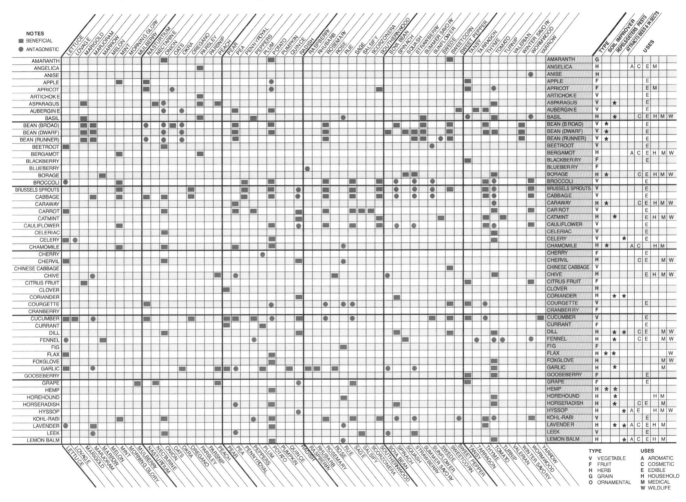

NOTES
- ■ BENEFICIAL
- ● ANTAGONISTIC

TYPE
V	VEGETABLE
F	FRUIT
H	HERB
G	GRAIN
O	ORNAMENTAL

USES
A	AROMATIC
C	COSMETIC
E	EDIBLE
H	HOUSEHOLD
M	MEDICAL
W	WILDLIFE

Companion Planting Chart © Michael Littlewood

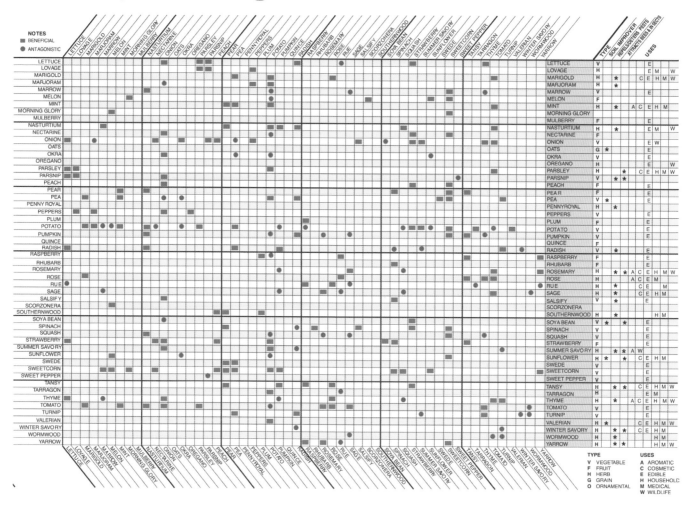

NOTES
- ■ BENEFICIAL
- ● ANTAGONISTIC

TYPE
- V VEGETABLE
- F FRUIT
- H HERB
- G GRAIN
- O ORNAMENTAL

USES
- A AROMATIC
- C COSMETIC
- E EDIBLE
- H HOUSEHOLD
- M MEDICAL
- W WILDLIFE

A companion-planted vegetable garden can be as ornamental as a conventional flower bed. Picture: Sally Cunningham

6 | COMPANION PLANTING IN PRACTICE

Companion planting encompasses a huge range of possibilities, and no gardener could – or would want to – employ all of its recommendations. Having acquainted yourself with all the options, you now need to take a step back and work out what aspects are appropriate for your garden, and helpful to you. Many specific plant pairings are relevant only to very dedicated gardeners, while others may or may not be useful – and in some instances there may be an easier way of addressing a problem.

For instance, one of the best-known associations is onions and carrots, with the aim of deterring carrot fly. This works – but only if you grow four times as many onions as carrots. If you do not have a use for that many onions, it may be more sensible to use another method of deterring carrot fly, like insect-proof mesh. Similarly, mulching the soil surface with organic matter can achieve the same aims as underplanting, and may involve less work.

Be aware that many of the planting associations which are recommended are not underpinned by scientific research. Companion planting is a huge

Left: Scarlet flax Linum rubrum – *here grown alongside parsnips – makes a good companion plant.*
Picture: Sally Cunningham

subject, and the research is only in its early stages. In the meantime, much of what is written on the subject is based on anecdote and hearsay, copied forward from one text to the next. Books are fond of saying that a particular pairing is 'good' or 'bad', with no explanation as to why, and advice is rarely given on what proportion of each plant is needed to be effective. This is one area where you need to experiment and find out for yourself what works in your garden.

Much of the advice is based on personal experience – and while personal experience is good, no one person, 'expert' or otherwise, can provide a definitive statement of what works. Many companion planting effects are specific to particular areas, soils, plant varieties or gardening styles, and what works in one garden may not work in yours. There may well have been other factors in play which do not apply to your garden.

It is important to remember that companion planting does not exist in isolation. There are many variables involved in successful gardening, notably soil, fertility, light, water, weather, climate, lunar cycles – and the skill of the gardener. A companion planting association may protect against a particular pest in a year when it is scarce, and be inadequate in a year when it is abundant. You should not rely on companion planting alone to protect a valued

First principles of companion gardening

- *Decide which aspects of companion planting are appropriate for your garden.*

- *Choose a style of companion planting to suit your style of gardening.*

- *Keep your planting as mixed as possible, while following a crop rotation.*

- *Start by introducing general companion planting techniques, like growing insect-attracting flowers.*

- *Use companion planting alongside other organic techniques; do not rely on it alone.*

- *Plan your companion garden on paper first.*

- *Monitor your companion planting systems to avoid negative effects like competition between plants.*

- *Do not believe everything you read!*

- *Experiment to find out what works in your garden.*

crop from a likely pest; be vigilant, and have additional measures on stand-by.

Success with companion planting often depends on the relative proportions of the plants involved, their relative sowing times, and their proximity to one another. Plant too few of a companion crop and it will have little or no effect; plant too much and it will outcompete your crop for light, water and nutrients. Although companion planting seeks to mimic natural growing systems, it is important to remember that, in nature, not all plants prosper. Some become dominant; others die out. In a garden, where we want all our plants to succeed, we need to monitor and manage our mixed planting systems.

Where you are interplanting two or more crops, it is essential that you give both (or all) of them sufficient space. Where you are growing a companion plant amongst or alongside a crop, make sure that it is not going to encroach on the crop's growing space. If you are underplanting, wait until the crop is established before sowing the companion, or sow seeds around young plants at planting-out time. And if, despite all that, a companion looks to be overwhelming the crop it was planted to support, remove it.

It is helpful – with any kind of garden – to sit down and draw up a plan first, and this is especially the case where you are planning a companion garden. You will need to factor in extra space for companion crops and flowers; you may want to make room for borders around your vegetable beds, or to plant crops at wider than normal spacing to leave room for interplanting. Where you are following a crop rotation, but also want to grow specific crops together, you will need to weigh up the competing factors and work out the best way of laying out your crops. All of this is easier to plan on paper than on the ground.

If you are underplanting a companion plant like clover, it is essential to ensure that it does not outcompete your crop. Picture: Dave Bevan

7 | CONCLUSION

Companion planting can be incorporated into any style of edible gardening, whether it is the informality of the cottage garden, with its riotous bevy of intermingled fruit, flowers, herbs and vegetables, or the formality of the traditional vegetable garden, where crop rows can be separated by strips of companion herbs, or surrounded by flowers.

Companion planting is perfectly suited to an ornamental kitchen garden or potager, which naturally tends to a mixed style of planting, and where flowers and herbs amongst the vegetables will be decorative as well as beneficial. But if you prefer to keep a more traditional plot layout, companion flowers and herbs can instead be planted around the borders of your vegetable plots. Remember that native plants – otherwise known as weeds – can also function as valuable companions, attracting and nurturing beneficial insects, if you permit a few to flourish around the edges of your vegetable beds.

A first step would be to move from large blocks and long rows of single crops to a more mixed style of planting. Experiment with intercropping different vegetables; plant salad crops alternately with cabbages, for instance. Introduce insect-attracting companion flowers and herbs into your vegetable

Left: If you prefer a traditional plot layout, grow companion plants – these are dead nettles and marigolds – around the borders of a bed. Picture: Dave Bevan

plots, either between the crops or alongside them, and plant some 'repellent' herbs alongside crops particularly troubled by pests. Try growing garlic alongside crops that are prone to fungal diseases, or underplanting your brassicas with clover, and observe the results.

Do not get bogged down in the myriad possibilities of companion planting. Simply growing a wide range of plants, both edible and non-edible, is the best method for the health of the whole garden, as it helps to provide a diverse habitat for a wide range of insects, both good and bad. Chances are the natural system will then sort it all out!

It is not always clear why specific instances of companion planting work. Some are not (and may never be) scientifically proven – but it is a fact that this method of gardening produces happier plants and provides better pest and disease control than monoculture. Not everything will work in your garden, or be helpful to you – but you will also discover other planting associations that do work for you.

This guide is merely an introduction, and the further reading section lists a range of books that will develop your knowledge of the subject and suggest yet more avenues for exploration. The possibilities for experimentation are endless, and one of the joys of companion planting is that one size does not fit all. The answers – the ones that work for you, and for your garden – are there to be discovered.

Further reading

A-Z of Companion Planting Allardice, Pamela (Cassell, 1993)

Companion Planting Bird, Richard (Quarto Publishing, 1990; paperback edition 1998)

Great Garden Companions Cunningham, Sally Jane (Rodale Press, 1998; paperback edition 2006)

Bob Flowerdew's Complete Book of Companion Gardening Flowerdew, Bob (Kyle Cathie, 1993; revised edition 2004)

Companion Planting Franck, Gertrud (Thorsons, 1983)

Primer of Companion Planting Gregg, Richard (Bio-Dynamic Association, 1981; paperback edition 2009)

Forest Gardening Hart, Robert (Green Books, 1991; paperback edition 1996)

Designing and Maintaining Your Edible Landscape Naturally Kourik, Robert (Metamorphic Press, 1986; paperback edition 2004)

Secrets of Companion Planting Little, Brenda (Silverleaf Press, 2007)

Companion Planting Little, Brenda (New Holland Publishers, 2008)

Introduction to Permaculture Mollison, Bill (Tagari Publications, 1991; paperback edition 1994)

Companion Plants and How to Use Them Philbrick, Helen & Gregg, Richard (The Devil-Adair Company, 1974; paperback edition 1991)

Carrots Love Tomatoes Riotte, Louise (Storey Books, 1975; paperback edition 1998)

Companion Planting Roberts, Margaret (Briza, 2007)

Bio-Dynamic Gardening Soper, John (Bio-Dynamic Association, 1983; paperback edition 1996)

Acknowledgments

*I am very grateful to the following people who helped to make this publication possible but my thanks go especially to **Gaby Bartai** for her writing and editing and to **Andrew Crane** for his layout and graphics.*

*Thanks to **Sally Cunningham** and **Elspeth Thompson** for reading the manuscript so willingly and promptly. Thanks also to **Garden Organic** for allowing me to take photographs of the Biodynamic Garden. Thanks also to **Cockington Court Kitchen Garden** for allowing use of their photographs.*

*I also thank **Sally Cunningham** for sending so many wonderful images for us to use and **Dave Bevan** for the images from his very extensive library.*

*Thanks too, to **Mike Hedges** and **Indra Starnes** of **Chase Organics**, for their support and encouragement.*